A Space Filled with Moving

Also by Maggie Anderson

POETRY
Years That Answer, 1980
Cold Comfort, 1986

CHAPBOOKS
The Great Horned Owl, 1979

A Space
Filled
with Moving

MAGGIE ANDERSON

University of Pittsburgh Press

Pittsburgh • London

The publication of this book is supported by grants from the National Endowment for the Arts in Washington, D.C., a Federal agency, and the Pennsylvania Council on the Arts.

Published by the University of Pittsburgh Press, Pittsburgh, Pa. 15260
Eurospan, London
Manufactured in the United States of America

Library of Congress Cataloging-in-Publication Data

Anderson, Maggie.

    A space filled with moving / Maggie Anderson.
      p.   cm. — (Pitt poetry series)
    ISBN 0-8229-3704-2. — ISBN 0-8229-5467-2 (pbk.)
    I. Title. II. Series.
    PS3551.N3745S6 1992   91-50759
    811'.54—dc20   CIP

A CIP catalogue record for this book is available from the British Library.

Some of these poems originally appeared in the following publications, sometimes in different versions: *American Poetry Review* ("Epistemological" and "Imperative"); *The American Voice* ("End of Summer in a Small Garden"); *Appalachian Heritage* ("Holding the Family Together"); *5 AM* ("The Invention of Pittsburgh," "Soup," and "Summer Solstice"); *Indiana Review* ("Doing My Part," "The Long Evenings," and "Setting Out"); *The Pennsylvania Review* ("Closed Mill," "Heart Labor," "Marginal," and "Ontological"); *Ploughshares* ("Gifts"); *Poetry East* ("As Long as I Can," "Anywhere but Here," under the title "The Memory of Venetian Evening," and "Wild Berries," under the title "Black Raspberries") and *The Women's Review of Books* ("A New Life" and "Big Romance").

"Pine Cone Boogie" was published in an edition of 1,000 as Winter Poetry Broadside No. 1 by the Kent State University Libraries for the Friends of the Libraries, Winter 1990.

I am grateful to the MacDowell Colony, Inc., the Pennsylvania Council on the Arts, and the Research Council of Kent State University for fellowships which assisted me in writing these poems.

Cover painting: *Above the Gravel Pit,* Emily Carr, 1937, oil on canvas. Collection: Vancouver Art Gallery, Emily Carr Trust.

In memory of my parents:
Frances DeLancy Anderson, 1908–1958
Orval James Anderson, 1915–1971

Think of anything, of cowboys, of movies, of detective stories, of anybody who goes anywhere or stays at home and is an American and you will realize that it is something strictly American to conceive a space that is filled with moving, a space of time that is filled always filled with moving . . .

—Gertrude Stein

Contents

Where I Live

I liked the place; I liked the idea of the place.
—Elizabeth Bishop

Ontological

This is going to cost you.
If you really want to hear a
country fiddle, you have to listen
hard, high up in its twang and needle.
You can't be running off like this,
all knotted up with yearning,
following some train whistle,
can't hang onto anything that way.
When you're looking for what's lost,
everything's a sign,
but you have to stay right up next to
the drawl and pull of the thing
you thought you wanted, had to
have it, could not live without it.
Honey, you will lose your beauty
and your handsome sweetie, this whine,
this agitation, the one you sent for
with your leather boots and your guitar.
The lonesome snag of barbed wire you have
wrapped around your heart is cash money,
honey, you will have to pay.

Epistemological

Facts situate us, and I know where I am
all the time. This is an alluvial plain
lowered by faults on the east and west edges.
The valley floor is never more than
twenty or thirty miles wide and through it,
the Willamette River flows north
to the Columbia and then the sea.

Or maybe not. I often get distracted
by clouds across this sky, blue as glacier water.
I mix them up with the range of mountains
to the east, or with surf blown far inland.
All this green picks up the reds for miles,
russet from the redbuds and the forest floor,
copper from the alders and the river.

Once I stood at the opening of an orchard
at dusk. How casually and certainly
we say things about the only world we know.
I was leaning against something ordinary,
a trash can, or a crate of yellow squash.
As far as I could see, row after row
of apple trees interlocked their gnarled branches
and cracked in the wind. When that orchard
opened to me, it warmed the air between us
and the soft ground rolled like an out-wave
pulling sand. There was a sound, like thunder
in a canyon, like a subway, like a drum.

If language can still mean anything at all,
this was what I used to like to call
the earth. And over there are shapes
in space called *branches, boughs,*
or *limbs*. A few hot miles below me
is a deep pocket along the Ring of Fire.

I get confused, the fir trees and the ryegrass,
the rocky coastline and the meadows,
but I know this slit in the earth,
this gash, this wound, where the burn
opens up and I slide in.

Empirical

Everything sad that ever happened to me
I have mourned beside a river.
This afternoon I sat by the bridge pilings
and studied the slow drawl of the Willamette
as it choked on the rocks and spit its current
back through the branches of cottonwoods.
Flood is easy for a river, like giving up.
What's hard is carving a valley, pulling
toward the sea on its hands and knees.

In my room there are twelve panes of glass
and beyond them a furnace of pink azaleas
pulling in the dark. It has been blue dusk
for some time now, and I have been watching
shadows alter these flowers to banked coals.

I lie down to wait for the river.
What I love about sorrow is its capacity
for metaphor, how sadness makes things
resemble each other. To the river, my body
is just a stone. I give it what I have,
first one, then the other of my empty hands.
It lifts and carries me a few feet
past blossoms of skunk cabbage, beautiful,
like sheaths of sun. I float for awhile
seeing clouds the way I saw them as a child.
My long hair trails behind me like a windsock
seining twigs and fish. At the bottom is
the vegetal mud, and it's not like anything
but it's mine. Like burning embers,
the azaleas suck up the dark earth
they fall to. I cloud the brown silk
of the river, and I take it in.

Not There

We saw it first as an absence,
what was missing along the span
of the High Cascades, the mountain's
aneurysm dissolved to still water.
We were driving in a green Toyota
through red pumice desert saying,
*That's amazing! You can see
right where it used to be.* And then
we looked down into what had once been
Mount Mazama and said, *It's blue.*

We read all the informational brochures:
two thousand feet down from the rim
of the caldera to the crater lake
and two thousand feet deeper down
to thermal springs beneath plumbed water
and a wind rising from it. We drove
to every viewpoint and recited the names:
black basalt, lava bed, fossil fumarole.
We got in and out of the car and stood
as close to the edge as we dared.

I believe this as much as I believe anything.
The ground beneath our feet was never stable,
and one language is as good as another
for describing what no one has ever seen.
Once this crater was high mountain.
Now it is blue kettle drum or magma chamber,
sinkhole or soup bowl, mouth of silver tuba.
We stared from as close as we allowed
ourselves to stand, three human beings,
who kept trying to talk about
the deep blue world that was not there.

Imperative

There was a grief I had to learn
by sitting quietly all afternoon
under fir trees pulling slats of light
down through heavy boughs in rain,
by watching clouds shift and swell
like tides in the uncertain sky of Oregon.

I love this little country road
that meanders from Corvallis to Eugene.
In early spring the soft blue-green
of the ryegrass overtakes the wide fields
they burned in autumn and ploughed under.
Along the fence line, daffodils are blooming
and through their yellow petals I can
glimpse the dark line of the river.

Not long ago, as if in fever,
white men hauled their plunder and truck
down into this green valley
to take up the work of clearing out
and settling, removing the stones
from the fields, and the timber,
the Siletz and the Siuslaw. How smooth
and clean they forced the silted basin,
how dense the cherry orchards
they have cultivated. It must have
seemed to them the promised land,
but even so, some of them would
give it up and go back home.

In this town, the church has
been abandoned. The grocery store burned
down long ago, and now the yellow tape
of the police line that barricades
the ashes has begun to fray and tear.

I could walk right through it
and stand among the charred boards,
poke through the damp debris,
the shattered glass and tin can lids.
I could pick around until I found
something solid to take home,
then I could carry it away.
This would be my privilege,
alone here, and the sun going down,
to walk freely with a stolen thing
beyond the empty barns and stables
out into the furrowed fields,
grief layered over grief,
I could let go of it or not,
at the edge of the river.

Beyond Even This

Who would have thought the afterlife would
look so much like Ohio? A small town place,
thickly settled among deciduous trees.
I lived for what seemed a very short time.
Several things did not work out.
Casually almost, I became another one
of the departed, but I had never imagined
the tunnel of hot wind that pulls
the newly dead into the dry Midwest
and plants us like corn. I am
not alone, but I am restless.
There is such sorrow in these geese
flying over, trying to find a place to land
in the miles and miles of parking lots
that once were soft wetlands. They seem
as puzzled as I am about where to be.
Often they glide, in what I guess is
a consultation with each other,
getting their bearings, as I do when
I stare out my window and count up
what I see. It's not much really:
one buckeye tree, three white frame houses,
one evergreen, five piles of yellow leaves.
This is not enough for any heaven I had
dreamed, but I am taking the long view.
There must be a backcountry of the beyond,
beyond even this and farther out,
past the dark smoky city on the shore
of Lake Erie, through the landlocked passages
to the Great Sweetwater Seas.

Marginal

This is where I live,
at the edge of this ploughed field
where sunlight catches meadow grasses
and turns them silver-yellow
like the tines of the birches
at the rim of the forest, where
lumps of earth are scabbed over
with rust colored pine needles
and one noisy crow has been
traversing them all morning.
Deep in these woods
his feathers have fallen so often
in some places they have started
to pile up like black snow.

I prefer it here, at the line
where the forest intersects
the field, where deer and groundhog
move back and forth to feed
and hide. On these juts and outcroppings
I can look both ways, moving
as that crow does, all gracelessness
and sway across the heaved up fields,
then tricky flight between
the overhanging branches he somehow
manages never to scrape against.
This life is not easy,
but wings mix up with leaves here,
like the moment when surf turns into
undertow or breaker, and I can
poise myself and hold
for a long time, profoundly
neither one place nor another.

Anywhere but Here

Memory's got its suitcase packed and is always leaving
whatever's right in front of it, the present moment,
which now holds pleated yellow dahlias
brushing my kitchen windowsill.
They look bewildered, like tourists,
mapping out rest stops and bending their heavy heads.
Last September I was a tourist myself,
bewildered and resting my feet
beside a souvenir vendor in black beret and undershirt
in Piazza San Marco, watching the pigeons pacing
the roof of the Ducal Palace and the ubiquitous tourists
lining up for gondola rides, while I waited for
a British tour guide to lead me out of Venice.
When a Greek steamer pulled into the basin
and announced itself, the pigeons whirred and lifted,
the tourists quieted their hundred languages,
and in the steamy lull that followed
the bells in the campanile sounded so American,
clanging with the ship horn like wind chimes
and traffic scored for pump organ, that I suddenly
remembered how, back home in Pennsylvania,
my dahlias would be blooming all alone where
I had planted them in the warm spring ground.
That was only homesickness, the sweet exile
of travel, but what shall I call this pang
I feel now as I reach to touch plush petals
here in my own backyard, heavy
and golden as Venetian evening sunlight
on marble bridges, leading me back
to green water, over water,
past the fondamenta's little barber poles
of piers, below balconies with louvered windows
opened into rooms with parquet floors
and who knows what other splendors?

Doing My Part

On the clear blue glaze of Lake Garda
eleven windsurfers line up their white sails
and tack toward Monte Baldo.
I could watch them for hours,
admiring their agility, their youth,
and what I imagine as their neo-Marxist politics.
They move south toward Sirmione,
The Caves of Catullus, which are not
really caves and were not really his.
Most likely, they were military storehouses
along the Via Gallica, but Catullus called Sirmione
"the eye of all islands," and he summered here
two thousand years ago, giving his imaginary lover
a thousand kisses. Italy has been having
its way with me, and today I do my part
by turning my back on the arteries of tunnels
Il Duce had built around this lake
to carry troops from Germany, while I oversee
the poetry these windsurfers are composing
as they tip over, tread water,
then haul their bodies up again
against the pull of billowed sails.

Heart Labor

When I work too hard and then lie down,
even my sleep is sad and all worn out.
You want me to name the specific sorrows?
They do not matter. You have your own.
Most of the people in the world
go out to work, day after day,
with their voices chained in their throats.
I am swimming a narrow, swift river.
Upstream, the clouds have already darkened
and deep blue holes I cannot see
churn up under the smooth flat rocks.
The Greeks have a word, *paropono,*
for the complaint without answer,
for how the heart labors, while
all the time our faces appear calm
enough to float through in the moonlight.

The Long Evenings

This far north in winter,
a scavenger daylight
picks its way across cold fields.
It comes from the sea
and the low clouds sifting
around the church spire's patina
and the bell tower windows.
It comes from the sea
to nose around
the icebound boats in Limfjord.
Here we sit in candlelight
that allows any stray emotion,
perhaps some old, still sweet,
indiscretion, or an anger
we thought we had no right to,
to come undone again
and spill across our faces
like the shadow of a wing
that falls, holding on
like a hungry lover, to what dark
there is inside this dark world.

Long Story

This is the midway between water and flame,
this is the road to take when you think of your country,
between the dam and the furnace, terminal.

—Muriel Rukeyser

A Place with Promise

Sometimes my affection for this place wavers.
I am poised between a vague ambition
and loyalty to what I've always loved,
kedged along inside my slow boat
by warp and anchor drag. But if I imagine
seeing this for the last time,
this scruff of the borders of West Virginia,
Pennsylvania, and Ohio, shaped by hills
and rivers, by poverty and coal,
then I think I could not bear to go,
would grab any stump or tree limb
and hold on for dear life.

I keep trying to say what I notice here
that's beautiful. There's the evening star
riding the purple selvage of the ridges,
and the flat shine of the Ohio where men
in folding chairs cast their lines out
toward the backwash of the barges.
There are the river names: the Allegheny,
the Monongahela, and the names of the tributaries,
Fish Creek, Little Beaver; the towns named
for function, Bridgeport, Martins Ferry,
or for what the early settlers must have
dreamed of, Prosperity and Amity.

Why can't we hold this landscape in our arms?
The nettle-tangled orchards given up on,
the broken fence posts with their tags
of wire, burdock taking over uncut fields,
the rusted tipples and the mills.
Sometimes I think it's possible
to wash the slag dust from the leaves
of sycamores and make them green, the way
as a child, after lesson and punishment,

I used to begin my life again.
I'd say a little "start" to myself
like the referees at races, then
on the same old scratchy car seat,
with the same parents on the same road,
I could live beyond damage and reproach,
in a place with such promise,
like any of the small farms among the wooded hills,
like any of the small towns starting up along the rivers.

Long Story

To speak in a flat voice
Is all that I can do.

—James Wright

I need to tell you that I live in a small town
in West Virginia you would not know about.
It is one of the places I think of as home.
When I go for a walk, I take my basset hound
whose sad eyes and ungainliness always draw
a crowd of children. She tolerates anything
that seems to be affection, so she lets the kids
put scarves and ski caps on her head
until she starts to resemble the women who have to dress
from rummage sales in poverty's mismatched polyester.

The dog and I trail the creek bank with the kids,
past clapboard row houses with Christmas seals
pasted to the windows as a decoration.
Inside, television glows around the vinyl chairs
and curled linoleum, and we watch someone old
perambulating to the kitchen on a shiny walker.
Up the hill in town, two stores have been
boarded up beside the youth center, and miners
with amputated limbs are loitering outside
the Heart and Hand. They wear Cat diesel caps
and spit into the street. The wind
carries on, whining through the alleys,
rustling down the sidewalks, agitating
leaves, and circling the courthouse steps
past the toothless Field sisters who lean
against the flagpole holding paper bags
of chestnuts they bring to town to sell.

History is one long story of what happened to us,
and its rhythms are local dialect and anecdote.

In West Virginia a good story takes awhile,
and if it has people in it, you have to swear
that it is true. I tell the kids the one about
my Uncle Craig who saw the mountain move
so quickly and so certainly it made the sun
stand in a different aspect to his little town
until it rearranged itself and settled down again.
This was his favorite story. When he got old,
he mixed it up with baseball games, his shift boss
pushing scabs through a picket line, the Masons
in white aprons at a funeral, but he remembered
everything that ever happened, and he knew how far
he lived from anywhere you would have heard of.

Anything that happens here has a lot of versions,
how to get from here to Logan twenty different ways.
The kids tell me convoluted country stories
full of snuff and bracken, about how long
they sat quiet in the deer blind with their fathers
waiting for the ten-point buck that got away.
They like to talk about the weather,
how the wind we're walking in means rain,
how the flood pushed cattle fifteen miles downriver.

These kids know mines like they know hound dogs
and how the sirens blow when something's wrong.
They know the blast, and the stories, how
the grown-ups drop whatever they are doing
to get out there. Story is shaped
by sound, and it structures what we know.
They told me this, and three of them
swore it was true, so I'll tell you
even though I know you do not know
this place, or how tight and dark the hills
pull in around the river and the railroad.

I'll say it as the children spoke it,
in the flat voice of my people:
down in Boone County, they sealed up
forty miners in a fire. The men who had come
to help tried and tried to get down to them,
but it was a big fire and there was danger,
so they had to turn around
and shovel them back in. All night long
they stood outside with useless picks and axes
in their hands, just staring at the drift mouth.
Here's the thing: what the sound must have been,
all those fire trucks and ambulances, the sirens,
and the women crying and screaming out
the names of their buried ones, who must have
called back up to them from deep inside
the burning mountain, right up to the end.

Sonnet for Her Labor

My Aunt Nita's kitchen was immaculate and dark,
and she was always bending to the sink
below the window where the shadows off the bulk
of Laurel Mountain rose up to the brink
of all the sky she saw from there. She clattered
pots on countertops wiped clean of coal dust,
fixed three meals a day, fried meat, mixed batter
for buckwheat cakes, hauled water, in what seemed lust
for labor. One March evening, after cleaning,
she lay down to rest and died. I can see Uncle Ed,
his fingers twined at his plate for the blessing;
my Uncle Craig leaning back, silent in red
galluses. No one said a word to her. All that food
and cleanliness. No one ever told her it was good.

Holding the Family Together

Near midnight, driving a sliver of backcountry road
between two steel cities, I remember the article
I read last week about the awful things that happen
to women out after dark in cars. Outside is only
forest and frozen creek bed, patches of black ice
on the highway, and "safety" has become
the soft melding of gears I'm counting on
to get me home. Thirty years ago, "home"
was only my father and I, eating our meals
in silence by the radio. I was as frightened then
as the small animals, whose eyes shine beside the road
my headlights illuminate, then flood with dark,
in a time so fast they cannot comprehend it.
My father said he was "holding the family together,"
the way Edith Piaf, singing now on the radio,
holds a song together through marching band music,
carousel rhythms, an abrupt modulation to a minor key.
C'était pas moi, I sing along, trying to make the dark
companionable, as I hit a pothole and command my tires
not to blow out here. If I needed help and if
it came, it would be another thing to fear,
like the knife blades my father
flashed through the yellow kitchen,
saying, *These, you see, could kill us both.*
Nothing to be afraid of, I lied to myself,
until he would quiet and tell me, *Listen
to the music.* Piaf's still singing
but I've gone rigid now with defense,
trusting to the wheel bearings and accelerator cable,
holding the family together, in my familiar
numb pantomime of a landscape, in which
no enemy could recognize me as his prey.

Celibate

In this fire, a place I used to live,
the three room apartment on Washington Mews
where one August morning I found
a pink rose dropped through the mail slot,
the limp petals of someone's whimsy.

In the riddled kindling beneath the grate
a few lit twigs curl and crumple
like bars of molten steel, poised
above cauldrons of industrial lava
along the Monongahela. Or how I imagined it
inside the miles and miles of mills
I once lived beside, where the barges
trawled their heavy loads downriver.

I could make this fire anywhere
by kicking at the embers I so carefully
scraped to the center of this pile of logs.
Maybe it's the place I'd like to live,
the windy coast of Denmark above the North Sea
where, in thirty years, the ocean
will have taken the white church, and where,
in a thousand years, the bulb of resin
on the fir log I'm lifting to the flames
might turn into yellow amber,
tossed and scoured by the tides.

I understand I could have touched you
as we walked through the cemetery
in early spring, among granite tombstones
lit to brass by the sun. There were
moments then, close and warm enough,
our bodies easy from the walking
and the cloying scent of lilacs and wild roses.
I understand that I did not.

I can find cornices of bark
inside this fire and shapes like gray topiary
where the smoke escapes. I have always
loved my hands and know them to be
beautiful, and my hair, how sometimes
its thick darkness grabs at light
and holds it like the fires
inside a tame volcano you might
hold your face to if I'd let you,
like this small domestic blaze
screened in my living room,
burning down to soft cold ashes
on the still-warm bricks of the hearth.

Closed Mill

I'm not going to tell you everything,
like where I live and who I live with.
There are those for whom this would be
important, and once perhaps it was to me,
but I've walked through too many lives
this year, different from my own,
for a thing like that to matter much.
All you need to know
is that one rainy April afternoon,
exhausted from teaching six classes
of junior high school students,
I sat in my car at the top of a steep hill
in McKeesport, Pennsylvania and stared
for a long time at the closed mill.

"Death to Privilege," said Andrew Carnegie,
and then he opened up some libraries,
so that he might "repay his deep debt,"
so that light might shine on Pittsburgh's poor
and on the workers in the McKeesport Mill.
The huge scrap metal piles below me
pull light through the fog on the river
and take it in to rust in the rain.
Many of the children I taught today
were hungry. The strong men who are
their fathers hang out in the bar
across the street from the locked gates
of the mill, just as if they were still
laborers with lunch pails, released
weary and dirty at the shift change.

Suppose you were one of them?
Suppose, after twenty or thirty years,
you had no place to go all day
and no earned sleep to sink down into?

Most likely you would be there too,
drinking one beer after another,
talking politics with the bartender,
and at the end of the day
you'd go home, just as if you had
a paycheck, your body singing
with the pull and heave of imagined
machinery and heat. You'd talk mean
to your wife who would talk mean back,
your kids growing impatient and arbitrary,
way out of line. Who's to say you would not
become your father's image, the way any of us
assumes accidental gestures,
a tilt of the head, hard labor,
or the back of his hand?

From here the twisted lines of wire
make intricate cross-hatchings against
the sky, gray above the dark razed mill's red
pipe and yellow coals, silver coils of metal
heaped up and abandoned. Wall by wall,
they are tearing this structure down.
Probably we are not going to say
too much about it, having as we do
this beautiful reserve, like roses.

I'll say that those kids were hungry.
I would not dare to say the mill won't
open up again, as the men believe.
You will believe whatever you want to.
Once, philanthropy swept across our dying cities
like industrial smoke, and we took everything
it left and we were grateful, for art
and books, for work when we could get it.

Any minute now, the big doors buried under
scrap piles and the slag along this river
might just bang open and let us back inside
the steamy furnace that swallows us
and spits us out like food, or heat
that keeps us warm and quiet
inside our little cars in the rain.

Abandoned Farm, Central Pennsylvania

In the middle of my life,
orphaned, childless,
I am perched on a promontory
of genealogy, where branches
fade from the yellowed pages
and the farm goes back to the wild
where it came from.

I had always thought I'd come on this
the other way, from across the open fields,
the long approach to distant house and barn
sheltered by a grove of trees. Instead,
I have stumbled out of woodland
up against a vine-covered back porch
where twisted limbs of hickory and maple
are knocking back the eaves.
This was a good house:
wide-planked floors and hand-hewn timbers,
mortised and pegged in place,
and what's left of it is good house still,
the uprights plumb.

This farm is no one's property,
no one claims it, sees it
as kin do, through the eyes of the community.
Beyond the smear of wavy glass
is kitchen: dry midden piled
on the ample hearth, a table leaning
against the wall. I can lift that table
up in my mind and see them eating.
I can people my vision
and watch them in the fidgit of their tasks,
but I cannot make them speak to me
beyond the harsh monosyllables of tools
and work: *seeds, plough, cash,* and *crock;*
sons, and *wood,* and *hoe.*

*

The kitchen garden fences in
a stingy crop of blackberries between pickets.
Chamomile and dill still volunteer
among the wild mullein and cinquefoil.
This garden has become its own
ripe compost, fitted
like a bird's nest to its set of feathers.
Here is everything it needs:
mulch, and loam, and seeds sowed
by birds and wind to sprout at random.
Whatever grows is harvested
by groundhog and deer.

A shadow path leads to the ground cellar
where the dark smells like apples,
mildew, and potatoes. A mud-caked boot still
tramples down the reeds of broken baskets.
In this sarcophagus of thrift and dream,
a few cloudy Mason jars have exploded.
Glass shards stick to the moss,
and sweet preserves have splattered
on the door like clotted blood.

*

One year I thought I would visit
all the family graves and carry flowers,
tidy them like they used to do
on Decoration Day. I started
with my mother's family, weeding out
around the big granite headstone,
pulling ivy and pokeweed back
from my grandparents' chiseled names.
I swept, and placed wildflowers across
the mounds of dirt, telling myself I was
doing my duty to the dead.

But standing alone, the only living DeLancy
in the graveyard, I felt how outnumbered
I am by my kin on the other side,
the only one not yet come to the table.

I drove to where my parents lie
side by side in a modern cemetery.
Their graves are kept clean
with perpetual care, so there was nothing
for me to do. I sat down on top of one,
then the other. I wanted to see:
skulls and teeth, and water
pooling up in the wormy satin
of the boxes they were laid in.
I wanted to touch their hip sockets
and metatarsals, search out strands of hair
or threads of cloth. I am now
ten years younger than my mother was
when she died. I wanted to see
if time goes this fast under the ground,
if I could locate some trace of face
that looks like mine on my mother's bones.

*

Beyond the house the garden path widens out
to cattle road and gravel,
to the wide gabled doors of the banked barn
built into the hillside.
I had not imagined it so large,
nor the air so still, the floor
cluttered with pitchforks
and wheelbarrows, feed pails,
bedsprings, snakes of rotten rope.

In the regimented light
from vent slits shaped like sheafs of wheat,
I can see fine workings
of white oak beams, and a loft
of piled locust, cut and saved
for fence rail and door peg
and never used.

In my own house are the books and dishes,
the photographs, and cuff links in small boxes
lined with velvet willed to me by my family.
I worry who to leave them to.
Even sentiment wants function,
and some of these once-loved objects
have no more use, even to me,
than the tidy stalls below,
releasing their sweet stink
of moldy provender and stony dung
from the astringent masonry.

Barn swallows stir, racket out
from the thatchings of their nests.
A rusty rake rattles near my feet
with a curl and twist of black snake.
I freeze, then back out slowly,
the way I have learned to move warily
at the place where human habitation
has left off.

*

The scrubby meadow riffles with insect whir
and chicory. Maybe it was right
to have found the house and barn
before the fields, to see first
what passed for intimacy among this family.

Out here is what all the neighbors saw,
the public lap of their prosperity,
the bottomland of the Susquehanna River Valley,
rounded out into the elbows of the Alleghenies.
In the southwest corner, field stones
are piled against the windbreak.
An old potato digger leans, like a fussy child,
against crumpled wire fence.
I mount the sun-warmed grooves of seat
and lean onto the handles, just as if
I have known this movement all my life.

*

Who knows what the body can remember
from far back, through the blood
traces of habit and sweat?
In a little while I'm going home.
For now, I feel at ease,
a hermit crab, assuming my regency
of atmosphere and paraphernalia.

The woods are going to take this home place
back one day. And the dark hills will keep on
pushing and kneading this fertile valley down
as the river rinses it. A family lived here
for generations, and they were preoccupied,
like the rest of us, with food and sleep,
the unpredictability of weather.
I'm as at home as any of us
likes to think we are,
in our saving up for later,
in the solitary repetitions of our labors.

A New Life

I mean, however and wherever we are,
we must live as if we will never die.

—Nazim Hikmet

In Oregon

Early in the morning I eat a big breakfast
and walk through the Pioneer Cemetery in Oregon,
Eugene's first settlers' final resting place.
I've been unsettled here, unable to work.
In the wind the pine boughs seem to dance
in green quadrilles, something formal, maybe

a slow sarabande. It's difficult to say. Maybe
this is what fir trees do instead of breakfast:
they lift and lower their boughs in the dance
of the morning while everywhere in Oregon
people put on their raincoats and go to work.
How easily these huge trees take their place

in the gray fog and drizzle of this place
that has not loved me. I think it may be
because I only came out here to work,
and shallow rooted trees will break. Fast
cold rivers cut the mountains in Oregon
and shape this landscape, the way any dance

shapes the dancer. It's hard for me to dance
in this green cave, where I feel out of place
and out of sorts. What is it about Oregon
that makes me so edgy and off balance? Maybe
it's because, even just eating breakfast,
I get so intent on trying to make things work

that I forget my own home, the out-of-work
miners, the deciduous trees, the clog dance
of sweat-stomp and fiddle. I could breakfast
there in a truck stop at Cabin Creek, some place
where they talk like I do, familiar. Or maybe
it's not just homesick. It's possible it's Oregon,

this clear-cut, slash-burned country. Oregon,
to me, has too many men out fishing, and the work
I tried to do here fell apart. It's almost May, be
patient. In spring there will be a yellow dance,
they say, of daffodils and orchards, in this place
where what I anticipate most cheerfully is breakfast.

It's hard work to live in a place where the best
dance is maybe in the name itself. Beautiful.
Oregon, where a woman like me can break so fast.

Gifts

It turns out I was supposed to eat the blue Hubbard squash
I got for Christmas, lung-shaped refugee from the winter
closing of the farm market, relic of a profligate ambition.
My friend tied a red ribbon around its stem, and I thought
it was dying, so I mourned it. I found a place for it
in my kitchen, among the sunken cheeks of old potatoes,
the onions flaking filament onto the linoleum
where all January I have overseen its slow dissolve.

My mother believed that growing anything but vegetables
was decadent, and she always planted squash.
We had yellow summer squash cascading like geraniums
from the fire escape of the Bronx apartment, acorn squash
tumbling down the hilly backyard of the house in Englewood,
and zucchini I was sent to line up on the stoop of Bob Wernli,
the super in Fort Lee, who weighed three hundred pounds.
Those apartments fronted the George Washington Bridge
and maybe because of that, or because that was the last place
my mother was alive, I have these things confused: gardens
and my affection for lit suspension bridges, gifts and dying.

I see now I might have just prepared a nice dinner,
sliced the squash and sauteed it with onions and garlic,
but because I loved to watch the lights coming on over
the Hudson, summer nights when I lay sweating and waiting
for the flicker to take on the humid dusk and cool me down,
I thought I had to keen. I loved my mother too,
but only as a child does. I still needed things from her.
What she gave me that has lasted was all she knew
of vegetables and the name of every tree in New Jersey,
but at the end she was in a hurry, left some things out.

I have learned to love this dark entropic crucible:
this decaying squash, the orange sponge
that takes its tough hide over from the center.

But I have never known what to do with presents.
Still, I try to pay attention. I watch over things,
the way I watched for the span of lights, the bright city
on the other side of the river, and then for my mother
to be in her green car on that bridge driving home
years after she was gone. Anything you care to give
I'll lay down before me, a ploughed and empty field,
where, like my mother, I could face death
turned up like heavy stones from bottom soil
and where, unlike my mother, I am willing to plant
whatever one might reasonably expect to grow.

Soup

I make soup and name the seasonings:
parsley, the damp tears that,
homesick, I planted in the loved earth.
Tiny black pepper eyes. Mice in the walls,
the bullets we will have to bite,
sharp clove stars inside the blue pillow
I put over my feet every night
so nothing gets away. I add
sweet basil, mint or saint;
a small procession of bay leaf,
laurel. Salt stream, salt water,
sea anemone. The chatter of barnacles
stuck to the rocks, gull cry and kestrel.
Chicken carcass, soft bone marrow,
once feathered, this bed
for vegetables I know to speak to:
the riven onions, train whistle.
Limp celery stalks I hold up to the light
and try to see through, cold hands.
Potato skins, weathered leather,
cinched saddles and compost.
Rutabaga, sore toe, a sudden
drop in barometric pressure,
rich Minnesota farmland
where yellow leaves were swept
across the burned fields.
What floats through the blue air
is feathers, is white rice,
falling into pottage, into hunger,
wet snow that vanishes,
the steaming ground.

A New Life

Like the immigrant's lover who hates to travel,
my heart does not go everywhere with me,
does not always want its horizons broadened.
Now it has come back from the uncertain field
of its banishment, where I made it go lie down
while I was busy working, earning money.
It seems to me as sturdy as it ever was,
a granite boulder, a little rough on the top,
a little mossy on the north side, solid
as some bony shoulder I might lean on.
I imagine it is glad to see me.
Oh my heart, it's going to rain!
See, how the sky shakes stained clouds loose,
cooling this hot day down to gray pools
circling the pines? I am so pleased
you waited out my obligations. I'm here,
and for a little while, I'm staying put,
inventing a new life from what's at hand:
the susurration of the leaves, the black branches
turning, wet and shining. You're just in time.

The Invention of Pittsburgh

That was the year I drove around all the time
talking about poems. I'd eat my lunch in the car
between one public high school and another.
I was so exhausted, preoccupied with gearshifts
and poetry workshops. I forgot to pay
my income taxes and wandered around acting like
I was really earning what they were paying me.
That was the year Ed kept telling me
to eat more squid and, being accommodating,
I tried. I had to eat squid, gelatinous chalk dust,
in every Chinese restaurant in Philadelphia;
in New Hampshire, broiled squid, a double order,
no garnish, no rice. And once in Vermont,
I was so overwhelmed by all the multifoliate
deciduous trees that I ordered a squid sandwich
in a health food restaurant on Lake Bamboseen
that came to me on whole wheat bread with sprouts.
Then I was in Eugene, on a Saturday in February,
about four o'clock. I asked for a bowl of squid
in a little restaurant on Polk Street
but what I got looked exactly like Pittsburgh,
or the Pittsburgh I suddenly knew that I,
a forty-year-old poet sitting in Oregon
was about to invent from whimsy and weariness.
There were thirty bridges, and thirty highways
followed the rivers. Neighborhoods laced
the hillsides, through detours and freeway
construction around the inclines and concrete tubes,
circuiting the long walls of old mines buried under
the gray Carnegie libraries and the universities,
the closed mills and the steaming slag piles,
the orthodox churches on the North Side
where they bless the cabbages at Easter.
This is what the lonely imagination finds in
squid: the aftertaste of scallops, the texture

of cheap perfume, bright yellow leaves
on the sycamores in the parking lot
off Forbes, kids recumbent with radios
on the lawns of the robber barons' mansions,
intricate lingerie wadded up in a hotel sink
on the Boulevard of the Allies in Pittsburgh,
the tough, sweet city of the workers.

Big Romance

This spring my wildest love has been
the lilacs and the pink azaleas
blossoming in after dinner light
along the alleys. I love how
raindrops remain awhile
like pearls at the neckline
of the chemise of these geraniums,
and I dress up when I go out
to woo them with my dark hair
and my gentle hands. When I hold
this lavender and yellow-spotted
Korean rhododendron, it reminds me
of the open faces of healthy children
I have known, well-fed and clever,
in clean sneakers and little overalls.
I have totally surrendered to
the opulence of suburban shrubbery,
colors like the old hotels, magenta,
puce, red moon and orange of pumpkin pulp,
yellow of wild mustard, citronella.
Only the brightest ones draw bees,
but I am fickle and speak sweetly
even to the pale gardenias
throwing their cloying fragrance
indiscriminately over the warm air.
I would like to be a person they find
attractive, so I have gathered
all the fallen petals from the paths
and made a hat of them,
a hat I will wear like my heart
on my sleeve, foolish as I've grown
with love for flowers.

Pine Cone Boogie

I had been studying this pine cone
for some time, noticing how it teetered
on its branch, as if it might
be about to rise up into the melodies
the trees seemed determined to develop
out of the racket and the dither of the wind.
When it broke from the main bough,
it clattered down like wooden spoons
to arrive on the top of my white sneaker.

I admire its gumption,
the way it gathered itself up,
shrugged away the shuffle
in the leaves, kicked off all traces.
It reminds me of someone I wanted
to talk to who was busy, something
I was coming to know I was
looking for. What is the State to me?
Or the laws of art? Nothing interests me
as much right now as the resin
drying inside the drawers,
the sharp petals of this pine cone.

We are liable to love anything,
even this warty artichoke,
this aggregate of pitch and ganglia
I want to get lost with in the woods
among the ferns and fallen branches
fretted on the sandy path like green
guitars. I hold it to my ear and hear
its hum, so unpredictable, unlikely,

how it fell to me, pulling with it music
like none I have ever heard
from the strict harmonics of the pines
where I had been studying it for some time.

Good Time

If the hunger in your innuendo means
what I think it does, I like it.
You are not the one I love
but I'll give you a slow dance
to remember, this sweet hot tease
I trust you to resist, while my fingers
wander your spine to your neck
and I hold on, while your breath
insists its hint and sway
against the melody. I take my time
moving back from the rough kisses
I am not going to give you.
We are near enough and eager,
but it's clear you desire my elegant
reluctance, and in this way
we understand each other, lover,
your red scarf across my shoulder,
my buffed thigh against your knee.

—Maggie Anderson,
 A Space Filled with Moving

Wild Berries

The warm and uncut fields above the house
opened out in the afternoon
like yellow petals of loosestrife
as the jarflies fluttered
in the soft palaver of the breeze,
and I waded snakey meadow grass
to root out thickets
of wild black raspberries, tangled
among choke cherry and greenbrier.
The air cooled as I passed
into the woods and stood
in the flickering light above
little umbrellas of mayapples.
Two thin blackberry vines trailed
across the shifting stones
of the old smokehouse, and I ate three
handfuls, let a few more go, before
I crouched beneath the falling roof,
crossed under, and started down
the steep hillside's tarpaulin
of winter-soaked, rotten leaves.

Beneath the wide mittens
of sassafras, I caught the swift
propulsion of descent
in the crotches of hackberry
and beech, trapezing from branch
to branch of low-hanging maples, down
to the dry creek bed where I looked back
up at the cut and switch
of light through moving leaves.
I followed the murmur of water
up the neck of the hollow
to where the mountain's froth
churned against the rocks,

then pulled up the other side,
through oaks and lightning-struck
limbs of poplars, arm over arm,
clutching loose vines,
pushing my knuckles flat to the ground.

Where I hauled up, there was sunlight
on an old logging road, scarred
with tire ruts pooled like ponds
and shimmering with false morels
and fiddlehead ferns. The slash
of clear-cut timber was coming back
in fireweed, and waxy white
blossoms of mountain laurel melted
down the hillside to the trail.
I walked to where the sun fell
flat and hot on an upland clearing
where the grasses caught the sunlight
red, and the towhees teased at me
from the broken fence line. There,
I found no black raspberries, only
scratchy, overripe pellets of blackberries
already picked over by the birds.

I trudged back out the log road
down to the untrustworthy bridge
and followed the stream to where the blacktop
meets the farm road, where the filth,
new-cut from the berm, had been bedded
down in the creek's dry sluice. There,
beneath layers of dead sumac, dogbane,
limp columbine and pennyroyal,
were hundreds of black raspberry vines,
none yet discovered by the birds,
and in full ripeness.

With luck's greed, I picked
until my fingers ached
from the precision of the movement
and the berries dropped one after another
into the coffee can. I bent and crawled,
then stumbled out, my hands splotched
with berry blood and brambles.
Then in the lighted kitchen,
I rolled the dough and stirred
the thick syrup. I poured the dark rain
of berries straight from the can
into the damp spread of the crust
and turned them with a wooden spoon.
I waited while the pie baked.
I waited while it cooled on the porch railing.
Then, in the white heavy air
of dew and evening, I ate.

Summer Solstice

I watch the shuffle of leaves
sorting out sky from the slow crawl
of sunlight up the bark of two tall elms.
How long is this day?
How impossible the project of the pines
to square the circle of light
I sit in, with the steady lift
and lower of their boughs.
As if the bracken had been given voice,
a crow calls out and rises.
If this were the end, would I sit up
with an immense alertness
and ask for three more days?
Among so many trees, I imagine
I am a tree myself, a sycamore
struck by lightning, charred bark
curling to the duff.
Raw to weather and desire,
I am pared down to nerve and fever.
I watch the light and wait
for the year to turn me over.

As Long as I Can

The tall red dahlias have arrived
like a crowd of Anabaptists
ready to expel the Lutherans
and burn up their bills and contracts.
All afternoon I've been outside
trying to invent their similes.
Sometimes they look like second graders,
flummoxed by the end of summer,
staked to their desks. Or rain-soaked
scarecrows, reduced to only hair
and a dark center of eye.
This has been the last warm day.
When I riffle through the petals of one
blossom the size of an infant's head,
I can see mortality's brown wound
already festering at the edges,
so I'm going to cut this one
and carry it inside with me
to watch it fade. I will coffin it
in the silver salver where it will
float on oily water, releasing the sweet
perfumes of its anarchic fire.

Setting Out

Days like this I can't imagine death as
any more compelling than the man in the tollbooth
on the George Washington Bridge where, as a child,
I thought there was a lane for the dying
down which my mother chose to go, quietly accepting
her designated token and setting out
across the lighted necklace of the Hudson,
draped above its sludge and juts of pier.
My walk today was not this risky,
but maybe as theatrical, with September light
drawing in its purple sashes bit by bit
through the cutwork of the trees.
The sky held only cat-shaped and bosomy white clouds
like the ones children color, and I walked
the back road to the meadow, where I admired
the smattering of blue asters among daisies,
where two yellow Monarchs were doing dips
and quick dissolves. There was a bustle of travel,
in the jarflies circuiting the heated grasses,
the birds in rehearsal for departure, lining up
in parallelograms that lifted and then luffed
a silent V of backwashed wind. It was so quiet there
beside the brook, where the dog lay down with me,
relaxed as an old loafer in the sun,
which picked up the red in her fur and made
a kind of halo around her ears, so she seemed
a fallen angel dog, exhausted from chasing shadows
down the asphalt road. If I'm lucky,
I still have quite a few more years to live.
The goldenrod was waving its cabled lures
in the breeze, and I thought of my father,
his weak hands waving from his hospital window
where he stood, a shabby weed. He was calling out
to me, and I was far below him, hurrying off

to be with you. How could we have been so crazy
in love in the midst of all that grief?
Most of my walk today was leisure and delight,
no more than the usual cleats of sorrow
attaching to my heart, but even the most beautiful
of late summer days can cramp into a memory, uneasy
attention to what we haven't thought about in years,
like the wrong mother's hand in the shopping line.
We hold it until we feel the strangeness, then
let go, a little frightened, a little embarrassed
to have done this thing, caught off balance,
like the quiet leafy path I just now turned to
and surprised myself by starting to walk down.

End of Summer in a Small Garden

Whatever may have suffered from my neglect
will have to bear it. The accidents of weather
are over, and this year's fret and harvest.
Gray cornstalks crumple in the bunting
of their tassels, and the few green bulbs
left on the tomato plants will not get
sun warm enough to ripen them.
At night the deer come in from the forest
to savor the broccoli's last blue blossoms.

This is the autumn of my forty-second year,
and my friend, who is twenty years older than I am,
has a studied patience with my haste. She tells me,
Write what you know that you have not written yet.
She is learning to live wholly in the present.

Twenty years is nothing—
a splash of light, like crystal glasses tilted
in the pines. I have a circumspect attention now
to your footsteps across uneven ground. Still,
the buttery clumps of marigolds continue at the edge
of the garden, and the tall, wine-red cosmos
has just begun to bloom, pulling yellow flashes
of vireos in for the sweet nectar and seeds.
On this small plot of earth we walk together,
one warm September afternoon, beauty
fires up like brush in a sudden wind
that washes across our faces
and takes the tired waste into its arms.

Anything You Want, You Got It

And what will I say to my friend who is
twenty years younger than I am and who slows
her pace to walk with me along the path
the pines rained down on all afternoon?

Twenty years is everything—
your whole life, each leaf and fallen branch,
every random pile of stones. Tell me
what you want to do, your shapely plans,
and I will listen to your bravado. Everything
I have imagined was for you, for this hour
we rested in the warm meadow with the drowse
of bees and watched thin clouds rush over.

What I want to do with you is dance,
to saxophone and heavy bass, fast and easy,
the way ferns shift and lean toward sun,
or the way a thought starts up in pulse
and limbs. When the music slows and fades,
I will put my arms around you,
as I have in the dream from which
my own sounds woke me to gray morning,
and then, my dear one, you will turn
away from me, or I will let you go.

The Only Angel

I can see that, what with one thing and another,
you're all worn down, but you have to quit
calling out to me with all these elegies.
You're sweet, but it's clear you don't know shit
from shinola. I could bring you to your knees
with one hard kiss, but I want you to mother
up the good life, get around a little more.
You're trying too hard, hedging your bets.
I am not a porcelain light behind the trees.
You can't touch me. I'm not even here yet,
your heart attack, your wreck, your slow disease.
I am what you cannot know, the blank imposing door
that you will storm one day to get at me,
hot and ready, since you will have to be.

Notes

"Ontological" adapts the phrase ". . . when you go looking for what is lost, everything is a sign" from Eudora Welty's story "The Wide Net"

"Beyond Even This" is dedicated to Lynn Emanuel.

"Heart Labor" is dedicated to Tanya Agnostopoulou.

"A Place with Promise" is also the title of a novel by Edward Swift and I am indebted to him for the phrase.

"Long Story" begins with an epigraph from James Wright's "Speak."

"Closed Mill" quotes the motto on the Carnegie family coat of arms, "Death to Privilege." The direct quote from Andrew Carnegie in the second stanza of the poem is cited in Haniel Long's *Pittsburgh Memoranda*.

"Pine Cone Boogie" uses a line from one of Leslie Marmon Silko's letters to James Wright: "We are liable to love anything," *The Delicacy and Strength of Lace*.

"Wild Berries" is dedicated to Louise McNeill.

"End of Summer in a Small Garden" is dedicated to Jane Cooper.

"Anything You Want, You Got It" is a line from a song by Roy Orbison.

"The Only Angel" is dedicated to Jude Tallichet.

The sources for the epigraphs that appear with section titles and at the beginning of this book are as follows: Gertrude Stein ("The Gradual Making of the Making of Americans"); Elizabeth Bishop ("Santarém"); Muriel Rukeyser ("Power"); and Nazim Hikmet ("On Living"), translated by Randy Blasing and Mutlu Konuk.

About the Author

MAGGIE ANDERSON was born in New York City in 1948 and moved to West Virginia when she was thirteen years old. She has taught in the creative writing programs at the University of Pittsburgh, the Pennsylvania State University, the University of Oregon, and Hamilton College. She was coeditor of the poetry magazine, *Trellis* from 1971–1981 and in 1991 she edited *Hill Daughter,* new and selected poems of West Virginia poet Louise McNeill (Pittsburgh: University of Pittsburgh Press, 1991). Among her awards are fellowships in poetry from the National Endowment for the Arts, the Pennsylvania Council on the Arts and the MacDowell Colony. Currently Maggie Anderson teaches creative writing at Kent State University where she and Alex Gildzen are editing the anthology, *A Gathering of Poets,* to be published by the Kent State University Press in 1992.

Pitt Poetry Series

Ed Ochester, General Editor

Claribel Alegría, *Flowers from the Volcano*
Claribel Alegría, *Woman of the River*
Debra Allbery, *Walking Distance*
Maggie Anderson, *Cold Comfort*
Maggie Anderson, *A Space Filled with Moving*
Robin Becker, *Giacometti's Dog*
Siv Cedering, *Letters from the Floating World*
Lorna Dee Cervantes, *Emplumada*
Robert Coles, *A Festering Sweetness: Poems of American People*
Nancy Vieira Couto, *The Face in the Water*
Kate Daniels, *The Niobe Poems*
Kate Daniels, *The White Wave*
Toi Derricotte, *Captivity*
Sharon Doubiago, *South America Mi Hija*
Stuart Dybek, *Brass Knuckles*
Odysseus Elytis, *The Axion Esti*
Jane Flanders, *Timepiece*
Gary Gildner, *Blue Like the Heavens: New & Selected Poems*
Elton Glaser, *Color Photographs of the Ruins*
Barbara Helfgott Hyett, *In Evidence: Poems of the Liberation of Nazi
    Concentration Camps*
David Huddle, *Paper Boy*
Lawrence Joseph, *Curriculum Vitae*
Lawrence Joseph, *Shouting at No One*
Etheridge Knight, *The Essential Etheridge Knight*
Bill Knott, *Poems: 1963–1988*
Ted Kooser, *One World at a Time*
Ted Kooser, *Sure Signs: New and Selected Poems*
Larry Levis, *The Widening Spell of the Leaves*
Larry Levis, *Winter Stars*
Larry Levis, *Wrecking Crew*
Irene McKinney, *Six O'Clock Mine Report*
Archibald MacLeish, *The Great American Fourth of July Parade*
Peter Meinke, *Liquid Paper: New and Selected Poems*
Peter Meinke, *Night Watch on the Chesapeake*
Carol Muske, *Applause*
Carol Muske, *Wyndmere*
Leonard Nathan, *Carrying On: New & Selected Poems*
Sharon Olds, *Satan Says*
Alicia Suskin Ostriker, *Green Age*
Alicia Suskin Ostriker, *The Imaginary Lover*

Greg Pape, *Black Branches*
Greg Pape, *Storm Pattern*
Kathleen Peirce, *Mercy*
David Rivard, *Torque*
Liz Rosenberg, *The Fire Music*
Maxine Scates, *Toluca Street*
Richard Shelton, *Selected Poems, 1969–1981*
Peggy Shumaker, *The Circle of Totems*
Gary Soto, *Black Hair*
Gary Soto, *The Elements of San Joaquin*
Gary Soto, *The Tale of Sunlight*
Gary Soto, *Where Sparrows Work Hard*
Leslie Ullman, *Dreams by No One's Daughter*
Constance Urdang, *Alternative Lives*
Ronald Wallace, *The Makings of Happiness*
Ronald Wallace, *People and Dog in the Sun*
Belle Waring, *Refuge*
Michael S. Weaver, *My Father's Geography*
Robley Wilson, *Kingdoms of the Ordinary*
Robley Wilson, *A Pleasure Tree*
David Wojahn, *Glassworks*
David Wojahn, *Mystery Train*
Paul Zimmer, *Family Reunion: Selected and New Poems*